TOP CLASS

Grammar

Year 6

Now supported with CPD training
For info visit www.johnmurraycpd.co.uk

Hopscotch
A division of MA Education Ltd

John Murray

Hopscotch

A division of MA Education Ltd

Published by Hopscotch, a division of
MA Education, St Jude's Church,
Dulwich Road, London, SE24 0PB
www.hopscotchbooks.com
020 7738 5454

©2017 MA Education Ltd

Written by John Murray

Series designed by Claire Swaffield,
Fonthill Creative, 01722 717029

Cover illustration by Sara Anderton
www.catandfoxadventures.com

Associate Publisher: Angela Morano Shaw

ISBN 978-1-909860-12-4

Contents Page

Introduction

Top Class is a series that endeavours to combine traditional approaches to the teaching and learning of grammar, punctuation and vocabulary with new techniques and activities that support and encourage good learning.

The three core areas have been separated into three distinct books aimed primarily at Key Stage 2. The three books ought to be used in conjunction with each other in order to provide learners with a wider learning environment and for them to understand that these core elements of Literacy work together and are not to be applied in isolation.

Specific elements of the new Key Stage 3 National Curriculum have also been included in order to introduce Key Stage 2 learners to more complex grammatical constructions and vocabulary as they make their transition from attaining Level 4 to Level 5 in writing.

Each book, one for each Year group in Key Stage 2, aims to promote discussion about specific areas of Literacy and provide experiences and opportunities to use and apply what they have learnt.

The three books are as follows:

- **Top Class – Grammar**

- **Top Class – Punctuation**

- **Top Class – Vocabulary**

Each book contains lessons that develop a 'top-down' approach, allowing learners to see how we use language in context, not simply *when* we use a particular word, punctuation mark or grammatical construct but *how* to use it to its best effect when writing independently.

As such, it actively promotes the core principle that to learn grammar and punctuation well and to extend your personal vocabulary effectively, then you must not only see these particular elements of Literacy within authentic and meaningful context and settings but you must then have the opportunity to apply what you have understood in your own independent writing.

All too often children are taught grammar, punctuation and vocabulary with exercises that aren't rooted within an authentic experience; and, as a result, although they may gain full marks in their exercise books, they often misapply or omit what has been learnt in their own free writing.

The *Top Class* series seeks to address this problem using a three staged approach, each Lesson Plan being structured so that learners are encouraged to investigate and explore the English language; initially with support and guidance from their teacher and fellow peers before being asked to apply what they have learnt as individuals.

Think about...

Before undertaking the Guided activity, learners are asked about what they already know about a particular piece of punctuation or grammatical form and where they might have seen it.

This links directly to the Guided text, again helping learners to view grammar, punctuation and vocabulary in context, housing it so that stronger links can be made with prior learning and personal experiences. This can then be used as a springboard to explore and develop this further in a familiar setting.

For example, when looking at our use of capital letters when writing a proper noun, learners may be asked about why people use an atlas or map before looking at a tourist map of London and considering why place names and famous tourist attractions start with a capital letter.

Guided

This is a shared activity that engages the whole class.

Set within a specific and relevant genre of Literacy, it embeds each particular piece of grammar, punctuation or vocabulary being taught in a focused and meaningful way. Moreover, it invites learners to use this information in order to answer a series of questions that are related to the text itself and then begins to move beyond it.

Each of the three questions asked have been carefully formatted so that valuable practice for the end of *Key Stage 2 English grammar, punctuation and spelling test* can be undertaken throughout each Year group. Marks are also available so that pupils gain practice at providing fuller explanations for those questions where two or three marks are being awarded. Answers are provided on the Lesson Plan.

Independent

This activity can be completed as an individual, with a partner or within a small group.

Each Independent activity within the book is also differentiated at an upper and lower level* and offers teachers a range of practical activities that support learners as they practice what they have learnt in the Guided section.

Differentiated activities can be found on the CD Rom.

Homework

Included in this section is a homework activity that aims to encourage wider learning outside of the classroom to take place. There are two types of homework activities that are provided, each having been designed to help learners discover and engage with grammar, punctuation and vocabulary in the 'real' world:

A] Specific 'closed' questions may be asked in order that research skills, both modern and traditional, can be employed to find a particular answer.

For example: What is the capital city of Demark? Who was the first man to walk on the moon? When necessary, answers are provided on the Lesson Plan.

B] Wider 'open' tasks are given in order to afford learners the opportunity to explore the world around them and collect examples that are both pertinent and authentic.

For example, learners may be asked to find three examples where a shop's name uses an apostrophe in their local high street.

Extension

This final stage of the learning journey is an important one and underscores the importance of using a 'top-down' approach to the teaching and learning of grammar, punctuation and vocabulary.

Each Extension activity within the book is also differentiated at an upper and lower level.*

Its aim is to encourage children to apply what they have learnt in a meaningful and purposeful way in order to embed their learning.

For example, learners may be asked to write a shopping list when planning a party that will naturally include a colon or use strong adjectives to describe a certain event in a story.

More importantly, it is this *writing for purpose* (rather than to score arbitrary marks or achieve irrelevant ticks in an exercise book) that provides a meaningful opportunity for individuals to engage with the English language and create their own work that uses grammar, punctuation and vocabulary in a way that brings their work to life.

In this way, not only will each learner be encouraged to use particular forms of grammar, punctuation or vocabulary correctly but, essentially, they will gain a strong sense of

themselves taking an active role as a writer. It gives them a valuable sense of what it is like to be an author, one who uses grammar not only to improve the quality of their work but also to express themselves as best they can using the written word.

The journey from simply understanding how the English language works to being able to apply that knowledge in order to become a capable and confident writer is a journey that will continue into adulthood and one that, in all truthfulness, never really ends.

However, by providing meaningful activities for both the classroom and beyond, the *Top Class* series can help each and every writer to freely use grammar, punctuation and vocabulary to great effect and support them as they endeavour to bring the written word to life in order to inform, influence and entertain their readers.

Differentiated activities can be found on the CD Rom.

Plurals

Think about...
What do you know of Sinbad the Sailor?
From where do his tales originate?
How many voyages did he go on?
On his third voyage, he meets a cyclops:
What is special about this mythical creature?

Guided

You are being read part of the Arabian tale of Sinbad the Sailor.

This legend originates from the Middle East. Where is this? Find it on a world map. Indeed, at the start of his adventures, Sinbad is said to live in the city of Bagdad. In which country is this? Can you find it on the map? What does this tell us about how Sinbad and his crew would have looked like? Discuss your ideas with your teacher.

Once done, answer the questions on page 9.

Independent

You are focusing upon how to use and spell a variety of plurals, both regular and irregular.

On your own, with a partner or in a small group; complete the task sheet provided to you by your teacher on page 10.

Once finished, cut off the homework task to take home with you for further practice.

Extension

Retell this part of the Sinbad legend as tough you were one of his crew. Complete the task sheet on page 11.

Once completed, swap your story with a partner to proof read. Take care to check that your partner has used the singular and plural form correctly.

Answers

1 are trapped: Sinbad and his crew (plural)
are fearful: many more (plural)
is sealed: their fate (singular noun)

2 +self: singular (myself, yourself, himself, herself, itself)
+selves: plural (ourselves, yourselves, themselves)
himself, ourselves

3 scarfs/scarves, leaves, roofs thieves, chiefs, handkerchiefs/ handkerchieves
cliffs, dwarf/dwarves, lives

Homework

- December 23rd, 1958 (USA)
- $65,000
- Kerwin Matthews
- Stop-motion animation

Remember...
We use plurals when there is more than one of something.
This can be done in two ways:
regular: +s, +es, +ies, +ves
irregular: when the singular and plural
forms of the noun are spelt differently.

TOP CLASS - Grammar - Year 6

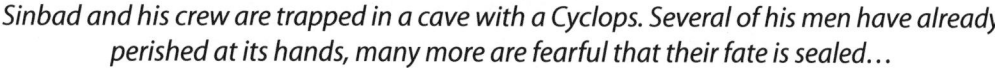

The Arabian Nights
By Andrew Lang

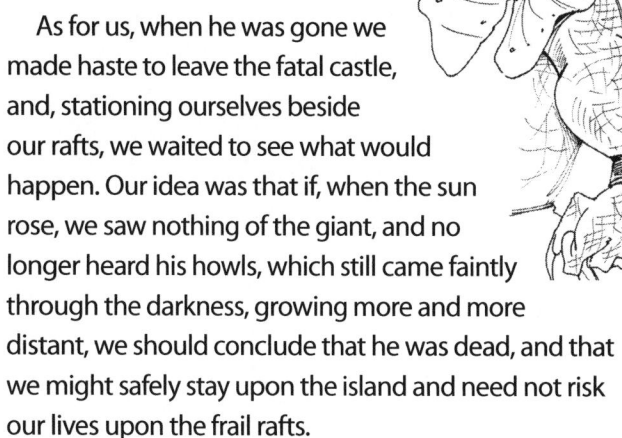

Sinbad and his crew are trapped in a cave with a Cyclops. Several of his men have already perished at its hands, many more are fearful that their fate is sealed…

Soon in came the cyclops, and one more of our number was sacrificed. But the time of our vengeance was at hand! As soon as he had finished his horrible repast he lay down to sleep as before, and when we heard him begin to snore I and nine of the boldest of my comrades, rose softly, and took each a spit, which we made red-hot in the fire, and then at a given signal we plunged it with one accord into the giant's eye, completely blinding him.

Uttering a terrible cry, he sprang to his feet clutching in all directions to try to seize one of us, but we had all fled different ways as soon as the deed was done, and thrown ourselves flat upon the ground in corners where he was not likely to touch us with his feet. After a vain search, he fumbled about till he found the door, and fled out of it howling frightfully.

As for us, when he was gone we made haste to leave the fatal castle, and, stationing ourselves beside our rafts, we waited to see what would happen. Our idea was that if, when the sun rose, we saw nothing of the giant, and no longer heard his howls, which still came faintly through the darkness, growing more and more distant, we should conclude that he was dead, and that we might safely stay upon the island and need not risk our lives upon the frail rafts.

But alas! Morning light showed us our enemy approaching us, supported on either hand by two giants nearly as large and fearful as himself, while a crowd of others followed close upon their heels. Hesitating no longer we clambered upon our rafts and rowed with all our might out to sea.

Read this Arabian legend and answer the questions below.

1 Read the introduction. Why are the following phrases used?

are trapped:	are fearful:	is sealed:

3 marks

2 When would you use the following two suffixes? Underline an example in the text.

+self: _____

+selves: _____

8 marks

3 Change the following nouns from singular to plural. Which rules apply?

scarf	leaf	roof
thief	chief	handkerchief
cliff	dwarf	life

9 marks

Plurals

Plurals can be tricky to spell, especially when they are irregular. For each noun listed below, find its plural in the word search. Put each one into a sentence of your own to show that you understand its meaning. When finished, use different nouns to create your own tricky word search.

Word Search:

S	E	X	O	B	H	M	O	S	A	D	D
E	X	T	R	J	M	E	S	B	B	Y	L
I	P	L	E	B	E	R	R	I	E	S	E
D	P	E	O	P	L	E	A	O	S	L	A
A	T	E	M	B	P	R	G	N	E	T	V
L	F	S	T	O	R	I	E	S	U	S	E
R	M	E	D	P	O	T	A	T	O	E	S
C	H	I	L	D	R	E	N	D	I	E	A
R	I	A	C	L	V	S	E	V	I	N	K
O	P	L	V	E	S	E	H	S	U	B	X
T	E	E	T	H	Y	F	O	X	E	S	M
R	T	C	H	U	R	C	H	E	S	E	Q

1. story   *stories* _____
2. box _____
3. leaf _____
4. mouse _____
5. child _____
6. lady _____
7. hero _____
8. tooth _____
9. berry _____
10. knife _____
11. church _____
12. fox _____
13. person _____
14. potato _____
15. bush _____

Homework

Find out about the film *The 7th Voyage of Sinbad* (1958).
- When was it first released?
- How much did it cost to make?
- Which actor portrayed Sinbad?
- Which type of animation was used?

You are a member of Sinbad's crew and have been imprisoned by the cyclops. While this monstrous beast is sleeping, you plan your escape. Write an account describing, in your own words, what happens next. How do you escape? Do all the crew survive?

Name:	Date:

The Cyclops

The beast was asleep. Several of our crew members had already succumbed to his evil appetite and we knew that if we did not escape, then our fate was sealed. There was not a minute to lose. Soon a plan was hatched that would deliver us from this monstrous brute.

_____

_____

_____

_____

_____

_____

_____

_____

_____

_____

Verbs & Nouns

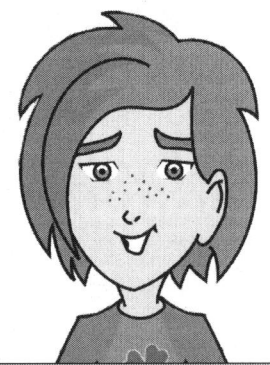

Think about...
Look at the following words:
**fish iron oil bandage rock
light stamp tick circle guard**
How are they both a noun and a verb?
Think of another example of your own.

Guided

You are looking up a recipe for baking apples.

How would baking an apple be different to stewing an apple? Have you ever baked an apple? How and why might you bake an apple if you were camping outdoors? As a group, make a list of equipment and ingredients you think you might need in order to create this culinary delight.

Once done, answer the questions on page 13.

Independent

You are focusing on the difference between nouns and verbs.

On your own, with a partner or in a small group; complete the task sheet provided to you by your teacher on page 14.

Once finished, cut off the homework task to take home with you for further practice.

Extension

Write a recipe of your own. Complete the task sheet on page 15.

Create a class recipe book full of your own, including colourful examples of the final product and easy to use instructions.

Answers

1 Core [N]: the hard, central part of some fruit that contains the seeds

Core [V]: to remove the core from a piece of fruit

2 Stuff [V], top[V], fire [V], place [V], crunch [N], hit [N], butter [N], mix [VN]

3 Allow for personal response. Discussion should also take place as to which terms might be found in a recipe book and which would not in order to clarify the differences in meaning.

Homework

- John Chapman
- September 26th, 1774 – March 18th 1845
- A barefoot pioneer apple farmer, who travelled America planting orchards as he went.
- His apples were not edible; they were used to make cider or Applejack.

Remember...
A **noun** is a person, place or thing. A **verb** is an action.
Sometimes a word can look the same as another but it can mean something else. We must look at these words within the whole sentence in order to work out whether it is a noun or a verb.

Baked Apples

Whether indoors in the oven or outdoors on the fire, this classic recipe will be a hit whatever the weather. Easy to prepare, easy to cook, even easier to eat! Three simple steps to deliciousness...

Preparation time: 6-8 minutes   **Cooking time:** 25-30 minutes

Ingredients: (per serving)
  1 cooking apple
  A handful of sultanas
  2 tsp of brown sugar
  1 tsp of cinnamon

Method:

1. Core each baking apple and discard the core. Place each one on a square of tin foil.
2. Mix together the sultanas, sugar and cinnamon. Stuff the mix into each apple and top with a knob of butter.
3. Wrap each individual apple in its blanket of foil and place in the oven at 200°C for twenty five minutes or until the apples are cooked through. Serve piping hot with vanilla ice cream.

   Tasty Tip: Mix it up a little by exchanging the sultanas for dried apricots. Adding flaked almonds or chopped walnuts will give your dessert that extra texture and crunch too.

Read this recipe and answer the questions below.

1 Why has the word 'core' been used twice in step one of this recipe?

I. _____

II. _____   `2 marks`

2 Are the following words in the recipe nouns [N] or verbs [V]?

stuff [ ]   top [ ]   fire [ ]   place [ ]   crunch [ ]   hit [ ]   butter [ ]   mix [ ]   `4 marks`

3 How are the following words both nouns and verbs?

whisk	chop	ice	season	toast	spoon
sugar	milk	jam	water	grate	dust

`6 marks`

Verbs & Nouns

Look at this list of food and drink:
water sprouts butter duck rolls flour milk fish
How can these nouns also be verbs?
Draw and act out each answer.
Now consider how the same applies to the words below.

Culinary Delights: Verb = (V) Noun = (N)

(V) whisk (N)	(V) cook (N)	(V) brush (N)	(V) crack (N)
(V) toast (N)	(V) box (N)	(V) cover (N)	(V) mix (N)
(V) cut (N)	(V) smoke (N)	(V) heat (N)	(V) ice (N)

Homework

Find out about the folk hero Johnny Appleseed.
♦ Who is this legend based upon?
♦ When did he live?
♦ What is he famous for?
♦ For what were his apples used?

You are creating a cookery book and want to include a recipe that uses apples. What will you bake?
Where does it come from?
What ingredients and equipment will you need?
How will you present your recipe so that the steps are easy to follow?

Name:

Date:

Preparation time:

Cooking time:

Ingredients:

Method:

Tasty Tip:

Modal Verbs

Think about...
Look at this phrase:
A dog's breakfast.
What do you think it means? Give an example.
Why might it have been used as a title?
What might it suggest about the text's genre?

Guided

You are reading a comedy.

Dad has been left in charge of making breakfast for two seven year olds, a baby and a Labrador. How hard could it be? What do you think will happen in this scene? If you were put in charge of making breakfast, how would you cope? Would it be an absolute triumph or an unmitigated disaster?

Once done, answer the questions on page 17.

Answers

1 A possibility

2 I. Permission:
II. Request:
III. Suggestion:
Allow for personal examples

3 A future time

Independent

You are focusing upon the use of modal verbs and the effect these have in relation to the possibility of an action occurring.

On your own, with a partner or in a small group; complete the task sheet provided to you by your teacher on page 18.

Once finished, cut off the homework task to take home with you for further practice.

Homework

- Newfoundland, Canada
- 10-12 years
- Height:
  Male: 57-62 cm
  Female: 55-60 cm
  Weight:
  Male: 29-36 kg
  Female: 25-32 kg
- Even tempered, gentle, kind trusting, agile, intelligent

Extension

Using the same title, create a comedy about someone who has been left the task of sorting out breakfast. Complete the task sheet on page 19.

Once complete, publish it on your class blog.

Remember...
A **modal verb** acts differently to ordinary verbs.
The most common modal verbs are: **will, would, should, could, may, can, shall, ought to, must** and **might**.
They often describe a possibility or an ability. They can also give advice, instruct or give permission.

The Dog's Breakfast

With mum in bed, Dad had been left in charge.
How hard could it be to feed two seven year olds, a baby and a Labrador?
Mum had left instructions but who needed instructions? Dad had this in the bag:
Scrambled eggs with tomato sauce smiley faces on toast for the twins... check.
A bowl of Fido's Best for Alice and a bowl of cold porridge for... hold on,
no that can't be right. Scrub that!
A bowl of cold porridge for Alice and a bowl of Fido's Best for Micky... check.
Mum would have to wait until after the school run.
A single phone call and the best laid plans began to unravel.
One fire alarm later and he was back:
Charred toast under the grill... check.
Tomato sauce decorating two school jumpers and the kitchen walls... check.
Cold porridge over a baby's head and Micky in the biscuit tin... check.
Mum stood in the doorway.
How hard could it be to feed two seven year olds,
a baby and a Labrador?

Read this comedy and answer the questions below.

1 How would you class the modal verb in the final sentence?

A request ☐   A possibility ☐   A suggestion ☐   A permission ☐

1 mark

2 How might you use this same modal verb in other ways?

I. Permission: _____

II. Request: _____

III. Suggestion: _____

3 marks

3 How would you class the modal verb in line eight?

A request ☐   A possibility ☐   A future time ☐   An intention ☐

1 mark

Modal Verbs

Underline the modal verb in each sentence.
Use the key to show how it is being used.
There are different examples for each one.
When you have finished, write an example of your own.

Key: Ability (red) Permission (yellow) Possibility (blue) Request (green) Advice (grey)

Could you pass me the salt, please?	◯	Take an umbrella, it might rain.	◯
It must be cold, it's snowing!	◯	The door wouldn't open.	◯
I wouldn't go that way, it's flooded.	◯	You <u>should</u> go and apologise.	⬤
Can we go swimming tomorrow?	◯	Couldn't we just email him?	◯
You're joking, Jack can play the piano?	◯	Can I leave a message, please?	◯
Side effects may include an upset stomach.	◯	We ought to say something.	◯
May I speak to the manager, please?	◯	Will you just shut up!	◯
She won't speak to you, she's too upset.	◯	He couldn't play football with his leg in plaster.	◯

Homework

Find out about Labradors.
* From where does this breed originate?
* What is its lifespan?
* How big does it grow to?
* What is its temperament like?

You are writing a comedy sketch entitled 'A Dog's Breakfast'. Mum has left instructions. How hard could it be to feed two seven year olds, a baby and a Labrador? Plan your sketch and act it out.

Name:	Date:

Act IV, Scene I

Setting:

Narrator:

Dad:

Narrator:

Dad:

Narrator:

Dad:

Narrator:

Dad:

Narrator:

Dad:

Adjectives I

Think about...
Do you know where Blackpool is?
Locate it on a map of the UK.
What is this seaside resort famous for?
Have you ever visited Blackpool Tower?
Compare it with the Eiffel Tower. What do you notice?

Guided

You are looking up some information about the history of Blackpool Tower.

In which part of the UK is Blackpool? Have you ever visited? When did Blackpool first become a holiday destination? Who for? Why was this possible and why did it became so popular so quickly? Why do you think Blackpool built its Tower? Why do you think it's still such a popular tourist attraction today?

Once done, answer the questions on page 21.

Independent

You are focusing upon how to select and use adjectives with increased proficiency and effectiveness to improve your writing.

On your own, with a partner or in a small group; complete the task sheet provided to you by your teacher on page 22.

Once finished, cut off the homework task to take home with you for further practice.

Extension

Write about a room of curiosities. Complete the task sheet on page 23.

Once complete, share your stories with your classmates.

Answers

1 magnificent

2 I. Parisian
II. metallic
III. Victorian

Discuss why answers I and III both begin with a capital letter yet answer II does not.

3 French, Danish, Swiss, Spanish, Belgian, Polish, German, Irish, Portuguese, Italian, Finnish, Dutch

Homework

- On the Champ de Mars in Paris, France
- 1889
- 320 meters (1050 feet) tall, it was the tallest man made structure in the world for 41 years until being surpassed by the Chrysler Building in New York.
- La dame de fer (meaning The Iron Lady)

Remember...
An **adjective** is a describing word. It gives us more details about a noun so that we can understand it better.
For example: its size, shape, age, colour, origin, material, opinion, observation and purpose.

BLACKPOOL TOWER

Built in 1894, Blackpool Tower is arguably the most iconic seaside building in the UK.
Yet there is no escaping the fact that if a Parisian were to visit the resort, they may well be mistaken for thinking they had returned back home!

A Grade One Listed Building - A Five Star Attraction!

★ The Tower was originally meant to stand 450 feet high. Once completed, it stood a magnificent 518 feet and 9 inches.

★ The Tower alone contains 2,493 tonnes of steel and 93 tonnes of cast iron. No wonder it takes seven years to paint this structure from top to bottom and replace any corroded steel work.

★ The original tender for the Tower was £42,000. However, when extra steel was needed to make it perfectly safe, this raised the figure an extra £23,000.

★ Each of the four legs of the Tower rest upon concrete foundations 35 feet square and 12 feet deep. This beast is going nowhere!

★ When first open, 10,000 light bulbs illuminated the Tower. Today these have been replaced by 25,000 eco-friendly LED lights.

What an Eiffel

In 1887 the Mayor of Blackpool visited France's capital. Impressed by what he saw, it inspired him to want to build a replica in his own back yard. Seven years later and his dreams had come true - Blackpool was home to its very own metallic monolith, one that towered over the Victorian promenade and dominated the skyline.

Read this leaflet and answer the questions below.

1 Find an adjective in the final section that means 'deserving to be admired'.

1 mark

2 Find an adjective that describes the following:

I. Someone from a specific city: _____

II. Something consisting of metal: _____

III. Anything belonging to the era 1937-1901: _____

3 mark

3 Which adjective would you use to describe someone from the following European countries?

France	Denmark	Switzerland	Spain	Belgium	Poland
Germany	Ireland	Portugal	Italy	Finland	Holland

6 marks

Adjectives I

Circle the adjectives in the sentences below.
Why might the writer have chosen these adjectives?
What do they tell us about the room and its objects?
What effect does this have upon the reader?
Draw and label each object.
Create a picture of the room itself.

The Room:

It had been some time since the room had received visitors and even now they were unwelcome.

1. Rusty hinges groaned as the door gave its reluctant permission to enter.

2. It took a while before their eyes grew accustomed to the dimly-lit room.

3. In one corner a grandfather clock bowed his head and did not speak.

4. In another corner a toothless piano slept on, dreaming of happier times.

5. A solemn portrait of Lady Chardonnay lay on the floor, its gilded frame chipped, dull.

6. Wooden boxes sat impatiently for their Master's return, their secrets locked from view.

7. A weather-beaten suitcase leant against the wall, exotic stamps telling of African safaris.

8. Sepia photographs decreed that joy had once lived here but had moved out long ago.

9. A newspaper, neatly-folded with faded print, spoke of a Titanic Disaster.

10. Fear gripped the bewildered visitors and refused to let go.

Place another object in the mysterious room?
What will it be? How will you describe it?

Homework

Find out about the Eiffel Tower.
 • Where is it located?
 • In which year was it constructed?
 • How tall is it?
 • What is its nickname?

You walk into a mysterious room, a room that has been hidden away for many years. The door closes behind you. As your eyes grow accustomed to the dark, you see many wondrous things. What do you see? How will you describe them?

Name: | **Date:**

THE ROOM OF CURIOSITIES

As I stepped inside, the door closed behind me. Silence. The darkness had swallowed me whole. I stood perfectly still, too scared to move forward, too curious to step back. I reached into my pocket, struck a match and lit the candle. Fear loosened its grip as the flame danced for joy and revealed the most beautiful of sights, sights that had lain hidden for many a year and from many a human gaze…

_____

_____

_____

_____

_____

_____

_____

_____

Adjectives II

Think about...
Where would you pick up a holiday brochure?
What is its purpose and target audience?
Why might it use a lot of adjectives?
How might it describe the following:
beach   sea   food   sights   nightlight

Guided

You are considering where to go on holiday in the summer.

Why might you want to visit an island? Do you know where the island of Rhodes is? Find it on a map. How would you get there? How long would it take? Which country's flag would it fly? Draw your answer. What do we call people who come from this country? With your teacher make a list of things people associate with Greece and its people.

Once done, answer the questions on page 25.

Independent

You are focusing on how to select and use adjectives with increased proficiency and effectiveness to improve your writing.

On your own, with a partner or in a small group; complete the task sheet provided to you by your teacher on page 26.

Once finished, cut off the homework task to take home with you for further practice.

Extension

You have been asked to write for One World Travel, a holiday company that specialises in providing the best holidays in the world. Complete the task sheet on page 27.

Once complete, create the page that will appear in its One World holiday brochure.

Answers

1 Greek: belonging to or relating to Greece, its people or its language
Grecian: as above especially of building styles or a person's appearance, in the style of Ancient Greece

2 sun-drenched beaches, chic restaurants, exquisite climate, quaint cobbled streets, authentic cuisine, vibrant nightlife, original character, huge Greek welcome

3 Allow for personal response ensuring that the main idea is why an author might use a particular adjective.

Homework

- Between 292 and 280 BC at the entrance to Rhodes' harbour
- The Greek Titan Helios (God of the sun)
- An earthquake in 226 BC
- The Statue of Liberty (USA)

Remember...
When describing a noun using more than one **adjective**, it is important that we place the describing words in the correct order before the noun. This is as follows: first size, then shape, followed by age, colour, origin, material, opinion, observation and purpose.

Rhodes

19

Escape that dull, drab Monday feeling and discover the jewel in the crown of the Greek islands that is Rhodes.

Its sheltered position in the Aegean Sea ensures an exquisite climate - this Grecian gem bathes in more sunshine than anywhere else in Greece.

Yet Greece's premier tourist destination has much more to offer than simply lazing on sun-drenched beaches or lounging by the pool. Steeped in history, the medieval area of Rhodes Town, with its chic restaurants and fashionable boutiques, has retained much of its original character. Losing yourself amongst the labyrinth of quaint cobbled streets is like leafing through the pages of time.

From the vibrant nightlife of Falaraki to the idyllic whitewashed buildings of Lindos, Rhodes truly does appeal to one and all.

With a huge Greek welcome awaiting you, not to mention the traditional tavernas and authentic cuisine, we are convinced that you will be captivated by the island's unforgettable beauty and charm and will want to return long before you have even left.

Read this holiday brochure and answer the questions below.

1 List and compare two adjectives that describe a person or thing belonging to Greece.

I. _____

II. _____

2 marks

2 Which adjectives does the writer use to describe the following aspects of Rhodes?

Its beaches: Its restaurants: Its climate: Its streets:

Its cuisine: Its nightlight: Its character: Its welcome:

8 marks

3 Why do you think the writer chooses each adjective? What effect does it have on the reader?

_____

_____

8 marks

Adjectives II

You are creating a website for a five star holiday destination. How will you persuade people to visit your resort and stay at your hotel?
Use the adjectives below to help you plan your writing.

★ ★ ★ ★ ★

picturesque

quaint

tranquil

chic

incredible

idyllic

modern

breathtaking

traditional

luxurious

exquisite

Beautiful

SPECTACULAR

enchanting

magnificent

authentic

superb

first-class

sun-kissed

fascinating

precious

vibrant

stunning

charming

historical

Homework

Find out about The Colossus of Rhodes.
- When and where was it built?
- Who was it a statue of?
- What destroyed this statue? When?
- Which statue is said to be The New Colossus?

You are creating a web page for One World Travel, a company that specialises in providing top class holidays. Where will you take them? Why would they want to go? How will you persuade them?

Name:

Date:

www.oneworldtravel.com

luxury holidays

One World Travel
Creating memories that you will treasure for life

Adverbs

Think about...
Look at the following sentence:
The doll lowered herself gently into the water.
Which word is the adverb? Circle it.
Why might the writer have chosen this adverb?
What does it suggest about A] the doll and B] the water?

Guided

You are sat around a campfire telling each other stories before you go to bed.

What genre of story is this most likely to be? Why do you think people like listening to and telling such stories when they are often so scary? If you were sat around a campfire at night in the woods, would you enjoy telling or listening to such a story? Why? Why not? This Tale of Terror is called The Doll. Why do you think such a simple title has been chosen?

Once done, answer the questions on page 29.

Independent

You are focusing upon why a writer might choose to use an adverb and why they might choose not to.

On your own, with a partner or in a small group; complete the task sheet provided to you by your teacher on page 30.

Once finished, cut off the homework task to take home with you for further practice.

Extension

Write a Tale of Terror of your own. Complete the task sheet on page 31.

Once complete, practice reading it to your classmates with the lights off and make them scared.

Answers

1 slowly – interestingly it describes an aching heartbeat which contrasts sharply with the quickening heartbeat of someone who is falling in love

2 perfectly – it emphasises the still silence that follows the twelfth chime

3 No – not all words ending +ly are adverbs. Here the word 'lonely' is an adjective used to describe the doll

Homework

- US President Theodore Roosevelt
- 1902
- Morris Mitchtom - at his candy shop in Brooklyn, New York USA
- November 14th

Remember...
An **adverb** modifies the meaning of a verb. It gives us more information about how, when, where or why an action is taking place. Usually an adverb will end +ly but this is not always the case.

THE DOLL

The old lady stood in the rain, her heart held captive by the lonely doll that sat in the window.

Her eyes looked empty.

Her lace wedding dress was moth-eaten, a smile that had faded many summers ago.

Perhaps it reminded the old lady of lost love, a love stolen from her on a beautiful summer's morn and never returned.

An aching heart beats slowly.

Whatever the reason, the old lady bought the doll and took it home.

Delicate hands placed her upon the mantel piece; undressed fingers straightened her hair and tidied her dress before going to bed.

The twelfth chime drifted away in the darkness… unheard…unnoticed.

Nothing stirred… a coffin of silence laying perfectly still.

The doll's head began to turn. Still her lips did not smile. Still her eyes looked empty.

She fell to the floor with a soft thud and began crawling towards the stairs.

Read this Tale of Terror and answer the questions below.

1 Find the adverb that describes the beat of the old woman's heart.

Why do you think it was chosen?

[   ]   [   ]

2 marks

2 Find an adverb used to emphasise the still silence of this scene.

[   ]   [   ]

2 marks

3 Is there an adverb in the opening sentence? Tick one box.

Yes ☐   No ☐

Why have you chosen this answer?

[   ]

2 marks

Adverbs

The most common type of adverb describes how an action is undertaken. They usually end with **+ly**. Create a host of adverbs from the words below and put each one in a sentence of your own.

How:

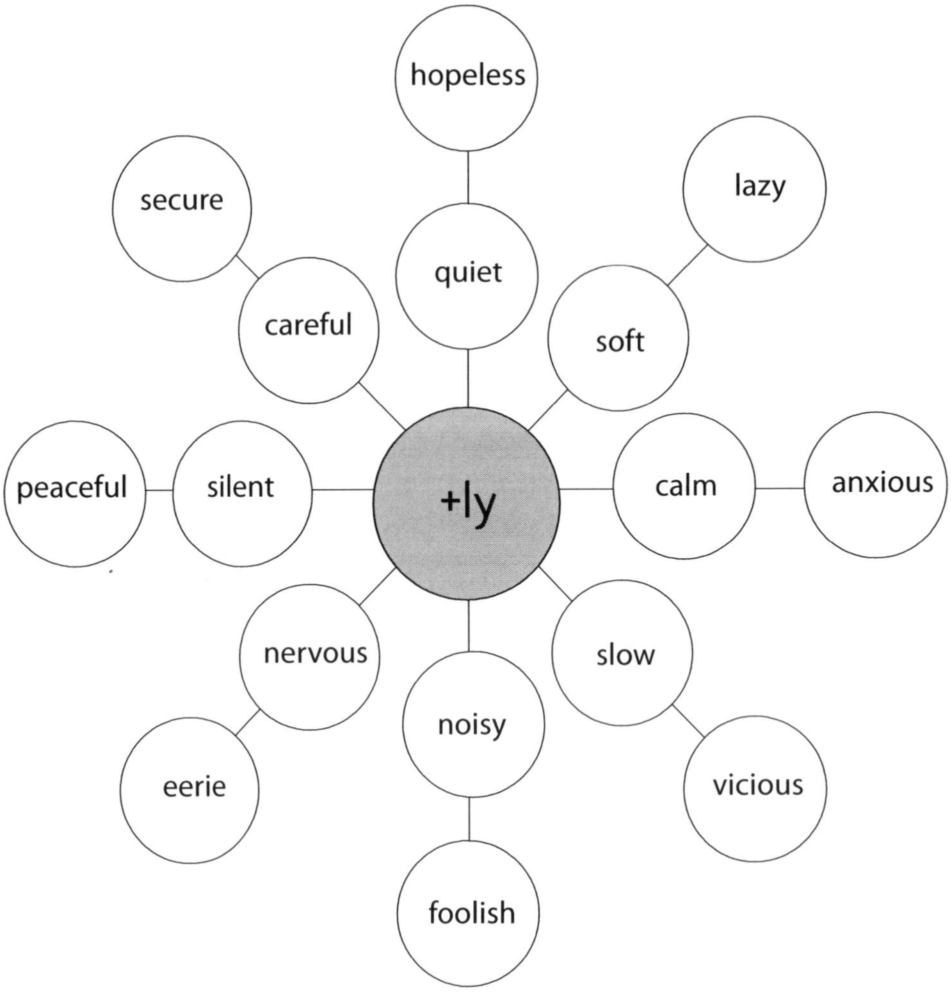

hopeless

secure

lazy

quiet

careful

soft

peaceful — silent — **+ly** — calm — anxious

nervous

slow

eerie

noisy

vicious

foolish

Homework

Find out about the origin of the Teddy bear.
* Who are Teddy bears named after?
* In which year were they first created?
* Who created the first Teddy? Where?
* On which date is World Teddy Bear Day?

You are sat around a campfire telling ghost stories. As the fire flickers and warms your face, you step from the shadows and begin your Tale of Terror. How will you make your tale terrifying? Will your friends ever be able to sleep again?

Name:	Date:

THE TOY BOX

It is midnight. The last of twelve chimes have faded away. Darkness reigns. For a while... nothing. Suddenly, a whisper breaks the silence and the toy box begins to stir; the lid begins to open.

The Continuous Form

Think about...
Who is your favourite storyteller?
Why do you like their storytelling?
Are you a good storyteller? Why? Why not?
Which aspects do you think you need to work upon?
Why might good storytelling be difficult?

Guided

You are considering what makes a good storyteller.

In pairs, list three things that you believe to be important when reading out loud. Put them in order of importance. Why have you put them in this order? Together with your teacher, consider how these individual ideas work together to create good storytelling. How important is this: A] for the listener and B] for the reader?

Once done, answer the questions on page 33.

Independent

You are focusing upon how best to bring a story to life when reading out loud.

On your own, with a partner or in a small group; complete the task sheet provided to you by your teacher on page 34.

Once finished, cut off the homework task to take home with you for further practice.

Extension

Choose an extract from a favourite book you have been reading. Complete the Task Sheet on page 35.

Practice reading this extract so that you can bring it alive using the prompt cards given to you by your teacher.

A copy of these reading prompts is available on the CD Rom.

Answers

1 Releasing: verb
Reading: verb
Happening: noun
Following: noun
(meaning 'the next')

2 Allow for variations:
A] We are speaking…
B] Mum was speaking…
C] I've been speaking…
D] They had been speaking…
E] Joe will be speaking…

3 Allow for personal responses (check verb tense agreement)

Homework

- No specific answers are required for this task, though teachers should provide opportunities for each learner to demonstrate the art of storytelling to a variety of audiences and using a wide range of texts, including those they have written themselves.

Remember...
The **continuous form** tells us that an action is taking place at that moment. We make the verb continuous by adding **+ing** to the verb. This can be used in lots of tenses: past, present and future so it is important we check that we are using the right one.

Great storytelling comes
from the heart.

A master storyteller breaths life
into the words held captive on the
page, releasing them into the abyss
of our imagination.

Whether reading alone or to an
audience of many, our storytelling
voice is important. It connects us
to the happening in the story, it
stirs our emotions and guides us as
we walk deeper into the text.

But which key aspects of our
voice should we consider when
storytelling?

The following ideas are by no
means exhaustive. However, they
do remind us of the crucial role
the storyteller has to play.

Pitch 🎵

How musical is your
voice?

Does your voice
rise and fall?

What tone do you use?
When?

Power 🔊

Volume:
How loud or quiet is
you voice? Why?

Can your audience
hear you?

Stress:
Which words are
emphasised? Why?

Pace 🏃

How fast do you
speak?

When do you speed up
or slow down?
Why is this?

Are the fastest readers
necessarily the best?

Punctuation ❗

Which marks do you
recognise?

How do they dictate
how you read?

Why has the writer
used them?

Pause ⏸

When should you
pause?

For how long ought
this to be?

For what purpose is
this?

Passion ♡

Can you emote the
words spoken?

Why is this vital?

Monotone = lacks
empathy & expression!

Read this advice and answer the questions below.

1 How would you categorise the following words in the continuous form?

releasing: _____   reading: _____

happening: _____   following: _____

4 marks

2 Complete the table using a variety of the continuous form. Use the verb to speak.

Present Continuous	Past Continuous	Present Perfect Continuous	Past Perfect Continuous	Future Continuous

5 marks

3 Choose two more verbs of your own to add to the table.

5 marks

The Continuous Form

Complete the table using a variety of the continuous form. Use the eight verbs in the table to help you. When finished, choose two verbs of your own.

You're Driving Me Mad!

+ing:	Present Continuous	Past Continuous	Present Perfect Continuous	Past Perfect Continuous	Future Continuous
drive	Dad is driving to the hospital as we speak.	I couldn't answer the phone, I was driving.	She hasn't been driving long, she's just passed her test.	Luckily, he had been driving slowly when the accident happened.	Mum will be driving us home, dad's too tired.
talk					
swim					
bake					
sleep					
read					
write					
run					

Homework

Don't just listen to a good storyteller, become one. The next time you enjoy what you are reading, pass on your passion. Choose somebody who would enjoy it too. Think carefully about how you can bring the words alive. Practice out loud beforehand and then give it a go.

The Continuous Form

You want to improve your storytelling. Take a book that you enjoy reading and practice reading it inside your head. When you are happy start reading it out loud, first to yourself and then to a friend.
How will you bring the words alive?
Use the cards below to help you.

Name:  **Date:**

Pitch

How musical is your voice?

Does your voice rise and fall?

What tone do you use? When?

Punctuation

Which marks do you recognise?

How do they dictate how you read?

Why has the writer used them?

Power

Volume:
How loud or quiet is you voice? Why?

Can your audience hear you?

Stress:
Which words are emphasised? Why?

Pause

When should you pause?

For how long ought this to be?

For what purpose is this?

Pace

How fast do you speak?

When do you speed up or slow down? Why is this?

Are the fastest readers necessarily the best?

Passion

Can you emote the words spoken?

Why is this vital?

Monotone = lacks empathy & expression!

Past Simple I

Think about...
Look at the following words:
enjoy time speak cut marry
love walk read worry buy
Put each word into the simple past.
How would you categorise them? Why?

Guided

You are considering how difficult it can be to write down a story in a set period of time.

Why might this be difficult for some and not for others? Do you personally find it hard? Why? Why not? What aspect of story writing do you find A] enjoyable and B] least enjoyable? Do you think it is important to be able to write a story within a set time? Why do you think teachers do this? Would you like to see this change? How might these changes improve your writing?

Once done, answer the questions on page 37.

Independent

You are focusing upon how to use and spell a variety of verbs using the simple past form, both regular and irregular.

On your own, with a partner or in a small group; complete the task sheet provided to you by your teacher on page 38.

Once finished, cut off the homework task to take home with you for further practice.

Extension

Write an anecdote about a happy time you spent being told a story. Complete the task sheet on page 39.

When written up present your anecdote to your class and include why you treasure this fond memory.

Answers

1 Paragraph 1: stuttered (R), stumbled (R)
Paragraph 2: came (I)
Paragraph 3: rang (I)
Paragraph 4: loved (R), packed (R) was (I)
Paragraph 5: could (I) approached (R)

2 As above – note also the regular spelling rules

3 Replace the y with an i +ed
Paragraph 8: try-tried

Homework

- No specific answers are required for this task, though teachers should check that each learner is able to articulate why they have chosen their favourite storyteller and demonstrate an understanding as to which aspects of their storytelling they believe makes them great.

Remember...
The **simple past** tells us that something happened in the past and is now over. This is done by changing the spelling of the verb in two ways: **regular**: +ed, +d, +ied or **irregular**: when the verb in the past tense is spelt differently and doesn't end in any of the three regular forms above.

The Story Teller

The pencil stuttered and stumbled across the page like someone fighting their way home against a punishing wind, stopping occasionally to catch their breath and gather their thoughts.

Jack came up for air.

"Ten minutes left," rang a familiar voice.

Jack loved stories. He'd close his eyes and let the words wash over him, let them carry him away to distant lands packed full of adventure and magic. It was his way of escaping the darkness.

His grandad had been an oak of a man. The place Jack could run to for shelter when storms approached.

Despite being unable to read, his grandad was the greatest of storytellers. His deep comforting voice would wrap around him, and help him set sail upon an ocean of dreams.

But dark clouds were gathering on the horizon. The air was chilled and there was nowhere to hide.

Jack's eyes became glassy. Some words on the page had become smudged, while others had now blurred into a fog. He tried hard to remember his grandad's voice, to hear his words. But another, less important voice drowned him out.

"Time over. Please put down your pencils. Make sure your name is on the front page before you hand it in."

Read this story and answer the questions below.

1 Find the simple past words in the following paragraphs:

Paragraph 1: _____ Paragraph 2: _____ Paragraph 3: _____

Paragraph 4: _____ Paragraph 5: _____

5 marks

2 Which of these are regular and which are irregular?

Regular: _____

Irregular: _____

2 marks

3 How do we change a verb that ends with +y into the simple past? Find an example in the text.

_____

2 marks

Past Simple I

Cut out the words below. Shuffle them and place them face down. Take turns with a partner to choose two cards. If the two verbs match (infinitive & simple past) keep them. Each pair must then identify the simple past word and put it into a sentence. The winner will have the most cards at the end.

It's all in the past:

chose	feel	slept	bit	knew
drank	wore	hide	thought	began
become	catch	blow	drink	fought
know	felt	speak	begin	became
blew	fight	bite	spoke	caught
choose	wear	sleep	hid	think

Homework

Write about the greatest storyteller you know.
- Who are they?
- When did you first listen to them? Where?
- What makes them such a good storyteller?
- What can you learn from them personally?

Think about a time when you were read a story.
What story was it? Who read it?
Why do you treasure this memory?
How did they make the story come alive?
What lessons in storytelling can you learn from them?

Name: **Date:**

Storytime

Treasured Memories

The Story Awakens

The Storyteller

Vibrant Lessons Learnt

The Story

Past Simple II

Think about...
Who was Tutankhamun?
Here is his supposed curse:
**"They who enter this sacred tomb,
shall swift be visited by wings of death."**
What you think this supposed curse means?

Guided

You are about to read the story of what many believe to be the first victim of King Tutankhamun's curse.

Why might King Tutankhamun have placed such a curse at the entrance of his burial chamber? What does this tell us about Ancient Egyptians? In fact, there is no evidence that such a curse was even found at the entrance. Many believe such curses are created by mixing an over-imagination with pure coincidence. What do you think?

Once done, answer the questions on page 41.

Independent

You are focusing upon how to use and spell a variety of verbs using the simple past form, both regular and irregular.

On your own, with a partner or in a small group; complete the task sheet provided to you by your teacher on page 42.

Once finished, cut off the homework task to take home with you for further practice.

Extension

Write an argument for and against people believing in the curse of Tutankhamun. Complete the task sheet on page 43.

Remember to include an introductory paragraph and a conclusion that includes what you personally believe.

Answers

1 searched: to look somewhere carefully in order to find something
scoured: to look somewhere very carefully (with great effort and over a long period of time)

2 ate, led

3 Regular: clutched, grabbed, arrived, died, reported, carried
Irregular: met, brought, told, left, found, spoke

Homework

- He began his reign when just 9 years old; he died when only 18.
- The Valley of the Kings, Luxor, Egypt
- The Egyptian Museum, Cairo, Egypt
- The beard fell off. After a botched attempt using glue by museum employees, it was finally restored by German experts using beeswax.

Remember...
When something that happened in the past is finished, we use the **simple past**. We show this by changing the spelling of the verb in two ways: **regular**: +ed, +d, +ied or **irregular**: when the past tense spelling of the verb is spelt differently.

THE CURSE OF TUTANKHAMUN

They who enter this sacred tomb shall swift be visited by wings of death.

For five years, archaeologist Howard Carter and his team searched for the burial chamber of Tutankhamun. Under the merciless watch of the Egyptian sun, they scoured the Valley of the Kings... but to no avail.

In 1922, Lord Carnarvon, who was financing the expedition, summoned Carter back to England to tell him the search was to be called off. Carter convinced his backer to support him for one more year of digging.

Upon his return to Egypt, Carter brought with him a canary.

"A golden bird!" Carter's foreman, Reis Ahmed, exclaimed. "It will lead us to the tomb!"

On November 4th that same year, the first of fifteen steps that led to the tomb of King Tutankhamun was discovered. The search was over.

That night, when Carter arrived home, he was met at the door by his servant. In his hand, he clutched a few yellow feathers. Eyes wide with fear, he reported that the canary had been killed by a cobra. A practical man, Carter told the servant to ensure that the snake was no longer in the house. The man grabbed Carter by the sleeve.

"The pharaoh's serpent ate the bird because it led us to the hidden tomb! You must not disturb the tomb!"

The Curse of Tutankhamun had begun.

Read about Tutankhamun's curse and answer the questions below.

1 Find and compare the two simple past words in paragraph one.

_____

_____
2 marks

2 List the two simple past words that Howard Carter's servant utters.

I. _____

II. _____
2 marks

3 Categorise the following words as regular or irregular when written in the simple past.

meet   bring   clutch   grab   tell   arrive

leave   die   find   speak   report   carry

6 marks

Past Simple II

The curse of Tutankhamun has struck once again! Use the verb cards to help you complete each sentence. Draw the Egyptian sign in the box, followed by the correct verb tense. When you have finished, use the same irregular past tense verbs to create sentences of your own.

The Curse Struck Midnight!

swim

ring

shine

sweep

freeze

1. The mummy [ ] _____ into a rage.

2. We [ ] _____ at the Temple of Anubis.

3. Lady Timperley [ ] _____ with fear.

4. The professor [ ] _____ perfectly still.

5. The telephone [ ] _____ but nobody answered.

6. As she [ ] _____ the candle, the shadows danced.

7. Panic [ ] _____ through the dusty streets.

8. The crocodile [ ] _____ in the Nile...unseen.

9. The gold [ ] _____ brightly in the velvety darkness.

10. 'A curse? Nonsense!' The boy [ ] _____ up the ancient scroll.

light

tear

stand

fly

meet

<u>Homework</u>

Find out about King Tutankhamun.
* Why is he known as The Boy King?
* Where is his body buried?
* Where is his famous Death Mask?
* What happened to the mask in August 2014?

What is the curse of Tutankhamun?
Where was it first found? What did it say?
Why do some believe the curse is true?
Why do others believe it is nonsense?
What do you personally believe and why?

Name:	Date:

THE CURSE OF TUTANKHAMUN: FACT OR FICTION?

Introduction:
What will your argument be about?
Why do some believe in such things and others not?

For:
What is the evidence to suggest that the curse of Tutankhamun might be true?

Against:
What is the evidence to suggest that the curse is superstitious nonsense?

Conclusion:
Sum up your ideas and present your personal opinion.

Present Perfect I

Think about...
Consider the title: **Shark Attack.**
What do you predict this text will be about?
A] Sharks that attack humans
B] Humans that attack sharks
After reading the text, did the answer surprise you?

Guided

You are reading a web article about the plight of the shark.

Why might humans hunt sharks? What will this mean for the shark population? Why is it important to consider the conservation of creatures that, in all probability, we will never encounter ourselves? How essential is it that we talk about endangered species and educate people about their plight? How might this education be best delivered and to who?

Once done, answer the questions on page 45.

Independent

You are focusing upon how to use the present perfect form with increased proficiency and effectiveness to improve your writing.

On your own, with a partner or in a small group; complete the task sheet provided to you by your teacher on page 46.

Once finished, cut off the homework task to take home with you for further practice.

Extension

Begin collecting some research on another endangered animal of your choice. Complete the task sheet on page 47.

Present the information to help raise awareness about the difficulties faced by the creature you have chosen and why they need protecting.

Answers

1 I. have plummeted
II. has become

2 Allow for personal response. However, answers need to show the difference between the plural and the singular form.

3 A] has proven   B] has begun
C] have learnt   D] has been

Homework

- No specific answers are required for this task, and teachers should encourage learners to present the information about their chosen endangered animal in a way of their own choosing. This will ensure a wider variety of creatures are discussed and presentation skills applied during the presentations themselves.

Remember...
We use the **present perfect** tense to express a past event that has present consequences. We form this tense as follows: **has/have + past participle.** For example: Call an ambulance, a snake **has bitten** me. I think I **have been poisoned.**

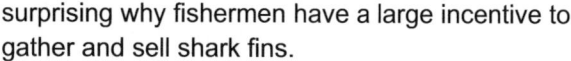

Shark Attack

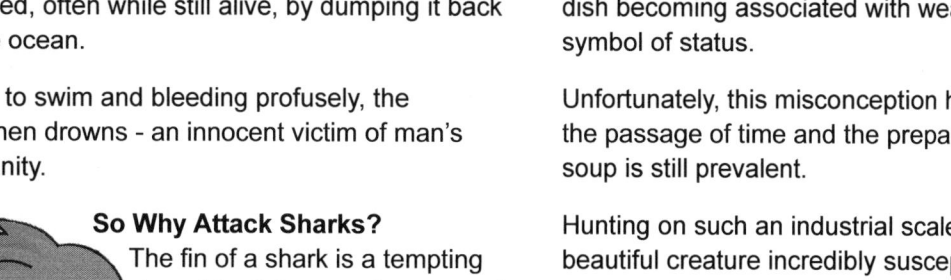

Although feared by many, shark attacks are incredibly rare. Indeed, these hunters have more to fear from us humans than we do of them. In recent times, shark numbers have plummeted, declining rapidly on a global scale - the hunter truly has become the hunted.

One reason for this is the practice known as shark finning, a barbaric process whereby a shark's fin is removed from its body and the rest of the shark is discarded, often while still alive, by dumping it back into the ocean.

Unable to swim and bleeding profusely, the shark then drowns - an innocent victim of man's inhumanity.

So Why Attack Sharks?
The fin of a shark is a tempting target for fishermen because of their high monetary and cultural value.

Selling at times for more than $500 a pound, it is hardly surprising why fishermen have a large incentive to gather and sell shark fins.

In the past, Chinese Emperors served shark fin soup to their honoured guests, in the misguided belief that it contained medicinal properties. This led to the dish becoming associated with wealth and power, a symbol of status.

Unfortunately, this misconception has not faded with the passage of time and the preparation of shark fin soup is still prevalent.

Hunting on such an industrial scale makes this beautiful creature incredibly susceptible to extinction.

The choice is stark: value what is important to our planet or loose it forever and endanger ourselves!

Read this article and answer the questions below.

1 Look at paragraph one. List the two examples of the present perfect form.

I. _____

II. _____

2 marks

2 Why does one example use **have** and the other use **has**?

I. _____

II. _____

2 marks

3 Complete these sentences using **have** or **has**.

A] Banning new ivory sales _____ proven to be a successful way of protecting Elephants.

B] An investigation into the theft of the collection of rare birds' eggs _____ begun.

C] The children _____ learnt a lot about the conservation of endangered animals.

D] The reintroduction of beavers in Britain _____ been controversial.

4 marks

Present Perfect I

Link the verbs together to form a chain.
Colour the past participle green.
When finished, choose some of your favourite ones and put them into a sentence of your own.

Have/Has + Past Participle

bit	thrown	steel	drink	bite	chosen
eat	done	hide	break	ate	torn
see	swum	fall	forget	take	drawn
speak	frozen	saw	fly	spoke	sung
drive	seen	throw	bitten	drove	sworn
know	ridden	do	eaten	knew	wrote
give	woken	swim	rung	gave	grew
write	took	freeze	spoken	drunk	taken
grow	threw	grown	driven	broken	drank
go	did	gone	known	forgotten	broke
choose	swam	went	given	flown	forgot
tear	froze	chose	written	stolen	flew
draw	rang	tore	ring	hidden	stole
sing	rode	drew	ride	fallen	hid
swear	woke	sang	wake	swore	fell

Have you ever seen an elephant? I've seen them on TV but I haven't seen a real one.

Homework

Find out about an endangered animal of your choice.
- Where does it live?
- Why is it endangered?
- What is being done to prevent its extinction?
- Can anything more be done before it's too late?

Research an endangered animal of your choice.
Why is this creature endangered?
How critical is the situation?
What can we do to prevent it from becoming extinct?
How will you present your work to ensure that your message is heard?

Name: | **Date:**

Present Perfect II

Think about...
A deadly plague arrives in your village.
You have two options:
A] Flee, save yourself but risk others.
B] Stay, risk yourself but save others.
Which option would you take? Why?

Guided

You are reading about the Derbyshire village of Eyam during The Plague.

Find the county of Derbyshire on a map of the UK. Where is Eyam located? There were an estimated 350 villagers who lived here in 1665, when the Black Death arrived on its doorstep. What do you already know about this terrible disease? How did it kill its victims? What do you think the villagers decided to do: flee or stay? Why might they have made this difficult decision? Were they right to do so?

Once done, answer the questions on page 49.

Independent

You are focusing upon how to use the present perfect form with increased proficiency and effectiveness to improve your writing.

On your own, with a partner or in a small group; complete the task sheet provided to you by your teacher on page 50.

Once finished, cut off the homework task to take home with you for further practice.

Extension

Imagine you were a villager of Eyam in 1665. Complete the task sheet on page 51.

When writing up your diary entry, try to make it look as authentic as possible by only using the writing equipment available to them at this time.

Answers

1 Paragraph One: have just been released
Paragraph Two: has claimed
Paragraph Three: has succumbed

2 Allow for personal response. However, answers must show an understanding of this tense together with when to use have and has.

3 Paragraph 7: it has run its course and its last victim has been claimed.

Homework

- Farm worker Abraham Morten
- November 1st, 1666
- Only 83
  (from a population of around 350)
- The final Sunday in August

Remember...
We use the **present perfect** tense to express a past event that has present consequences. We form this tense as follows: **has/have + past participle**. For example:
Call an ambulance, a tree **has fallen** on me and think I **have broken** my leg.

A parcel of cloth is delivered to the door of tailor George Viccars. Damp from its journey from the capital, it is hung in front of the hearth to dry. Unbeknownst to anyone, infected fleas have just been released into the quiet Derbyshire village of Eyam.

Less than a week later, on September 7th, George Viccars is dead. The Bubonic Plague has claimed its first victim.

Death stalks the village. Nobody is safe. By the end of the month a further five have succumbed, in October twenty-three more.

Talk is rife: shall we remain or shall we flee to the nearby city of Sheffield? A meeting is called by the rector, William Mompesson, and the village unites in their decision to stay within the confines of Eyam and contain the spread of the disease.

In recognition of their bravery, nearby parishes leave food and medical supplies on Boundary Stones to help sustain them.

Fourteen months limp by. Death continues its residency.

But by November 1st 1666, it has run its course and its last victim has been claimed.

Church records show that of the estimated 350 villagers, 273 died as a result of the unforgiving pestilence.

Nevertheless, such a courageous act of selflessness continues to be remembered, a poignant example of people paying the ultimate sacrifice for the benefit of others.

Read this historical narrative and answer the questions below.

1 Find an example of the present perfect tense in each of the first three paragraphs.

Paragraph One: Paragraph Two: Paragraph Three:

[ ]   [ ]   [ ]

3 marks

2 Why do you think each example has been used?

Paragraph One: _____

Paragraph Two: _____

Paragraph Three: _____

3 marks

3 There is one more paragraph that uses the present perfect tense. Which is it and how is it used?

[ ]   _____

2 marks

Present Perfect II

Use the past participle to create a question of your own. Answer that question in a positive and negative way. When finished, create more questions and answers of your own.

Have/Has + Past Participle

Verb (infinitive)	Question (?)	Answer (+)	Answer (-)
To steal	Has your necklace been stolen?	It's been stolen, call the police.	No it hasn't, it's in the safe.
To see			
To speak			
To ring			
To eat			
To know			
To take			
To write			
To give			
To ride			
To fly			
To forget			

Homework

Visit www.eyamplaguevillage.co.uk
* Who was the last plague victim of Eyam?
* On what date did he pass away?
* How many Eyam villagers survived?
* When does Eyam remember its heroic sacrifice?

The year is 1666. The Black Death is stalking the village. You return from a meeting where it has been decided not to flee so that nearby villages will be spared. Write in your diary how you feel when you return home.

Name:	Date:

May 1st 1666

Dear Diary,
Death continues to stalk the village. No soul is spared, despite our prayers.

Past Perfect

Think about...
What is a dilemma?
On a scale of 1-5, how hard is this choice?
Have you ever had to make a difficult choice?
Why was it such a hard decision to make?
Do you regret the decision you made? Why? Why not?

Guided

You are considering the dilemma of two people: a police constable and a thief.

Is it wrong to steal? From one viewpoint, the answer is both obvious and simple. However, there are times when such a viewpoint may not be as easy to make. Why might this be? Nevertheless, no matter what the situation, the law states that to steal is wrong and is punishable. Is it fair to always use this judgement when people might have stolen something in sheer desperation or need?

Once done, answer the questions on page 53.

Independent

You are focusing upon how to use the past perfect form with increased proficiency and effectiveness to improve your writing.

On your own, with a partner or in a small group; complete the task sheet provided to you by your teacher on page 54.

Once finished, cut off the homework task to take home with you for further practice.

Extension

Discuss the text's title in terms of the thief's dilemma before the theft took place and the policewoman's dilemma now that the thief has been caught.

Complete the Task Sheet on page 55.

Answers

1 had caught

2 I. had prevented
II. had not spoken
III. had asked
IV. had received
V. had taken

3 Rule: had + past participle
Allow for personal response.

Homework

- No specific answers are required for this task, though teachers should ensure that learners have considered both aspects of the dilemma before reaching their personal conclusion.

Remember...
We use the **past perfect** tense to show that a past event had already finished when another action happened. We form this tense as follows: **had + past participle**. For example: She **had spoken** to the police about security the week before the robbery.

The Dilemma

The police constable had caught the thief red-handed… an open and shut case.

Satisfied at a job well-done, she began studying the guilty man that stood before her.

Calloused hands and a weathered face spoke of a man who worked hard to provide for his family, cheap clothes and a tarnished wedding band told her that that work did not pay well. Yet he was clean-shaven, smartly dressed. He took pride in caring for himself and those around him.

She pondered the ease of his arrest… it was not his age or any infirmity that had prevented him from running, this man was stronger than even his frame would suggest.

He had not spoken and yet she sensed that his voice would be soft, gentle.

She wondered if that same voice had asked for help a thousand times and had only received the same answer, an answer that was followed by a long pause and an awkward apology.

She glanced at the pharmacist's window and back towards the man's blooded hand; hardly a professional. She stared at the label on the medicine bottle she had taken from him.

'Why?' she asked, though deep inside she already knew what the answer would be.

The man's lips trembled and were barely able to connect the two words together:

'For love,' came his reply.

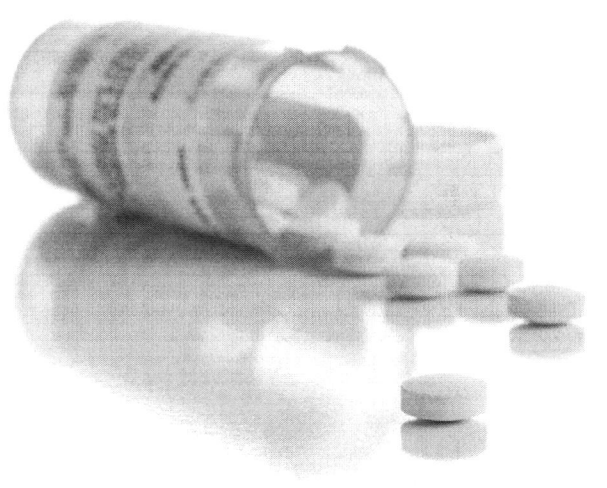

Read this dilemma and answer the questions below.

1 Find an example of the past perfect in the opening sentence.

_____ *1 mark*

2 There are five more within this story. Find them. Underline the negative form.

I. _____ II. _____ III. _____ IV. _____ V. _____ *5 marks*

3 What rule do you notice? Use this rule to create a sentence of your own.

Rule:

_____ *2 marks*

Past Perfect

Match the two parts of the sentence and connect them with either **so** or **because**. When you have completed both sentences, identify the past perfect tense in each one and circle it. How might you also make each sentence less formal? When finished think of two examples of your own.

Had + Past Participle

We had to take Fido to the vet.	He had to watch the match from the stand.	Lord Blackwell had called the police.	The athlete had to pull out of the London Marathon.	Ian had to borrow some money.	We had to take the long way around.
because			**so**		
Mum had forgotten to give him his packed lunch.	The storm had blown over a tree and blocked our path.	He had eaten some weed killer.	Someone had stolen the necklace.	He had broken his leg.	She had torn a muscle.

1a. He had to watch the match from the stand because he had broken his leg.	1b. He had broken his leg so he had to watch the match from the stand.
2a.	2b.
3a.	3b.
4a.	4b.
5a.	5b.
6a.	6b.
7a.	7b.
8a.	8b.

Homework

Think about the dilemma faced by each character.
- What do you think the old man's dilemma was?
- Why do you think he made his final decision?
- What do you think the policewoman's dilemma is?
- What do you think her decision will be? Why?

Look back at the dilemma you read on page 53. Think carefully about the dilemma each character faces. What dilemma did the old man face before he broke into the pharmacy? What dilemma might the police constable now face having worked out why the theft has taken place?

Name:

Date:

The Old Man's Dilemma

The Policewoman's Dilemma

Past Perfect Continuous

Think about...
Read the title of this chapter.
What does it imply about this planet?
What might the weather conditions be like?
Why else might it be unsafe to remain here?
With this in mind, who might read this book? Why?

Guided

You are reading a chapter from a sci-fi book.

What does the term sci-fi mean? Give an example of a sci-fi adventure film or television programme that you have seen? With this in mind, what might we expect to find in this text in terms of its characters, setting and storyline? Do you like this particular genre? Why? Why not? How might this colour your view of the text before you have even read it? Is this fair?

Once done, answer the questions on page 57.

Independent

You are focusing upon how to use the past perfect form with increased proficiency and effectiveness to improve your writing.

On your own, with a partner or in a small group; complete the task sheet provided to you by your teacher on page 58.

Once finished, cut off the homework task to take home with you for further practice.

Extension

Write the next part of this space adventure. Complete the Task Sheet on page 59.

When completed, design a book cover and blurb for this story.

Answers

1
I. had survived
II. had salvaged
III. had consumed
IV. had been received
V. <u>had not pursued</u>

2 Regular: The emergency sirens had ceased.

Irregular: The uprising had begun.

3 had been + past participle
Allow for personal examples.
A] had been searching
B] had not been fighting
C] had been struggling
D] had not been walking

Homework

- No specific answers are required for this task, though teachers should ensure that learners have included both the past perfect and past perfect continuous when writing the blurb for their book cover.

Remember...
We use the **past perfect** tense to show that a past event had already finished when another action happened. We form this tense as follows: **had + past participle**. For example: Luckily, the crew **had eaten** before they came under attack.

Past Perfect Continuous

Chapter IX
Escape from Elgin Minor

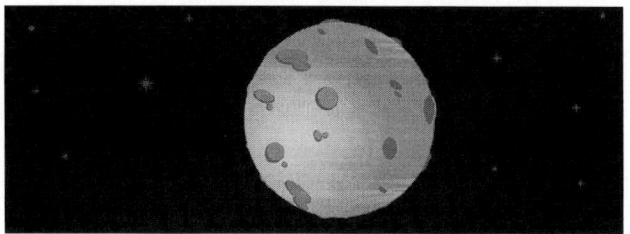

The carcass of the ship lay smouldering in the distance. Teller and his crew had survived the impact and had salvaged what they could before the fire had consumed any hope of shelter or escape.

All they could pray for now was that their distress call had been received by Jupiter Station and that a rescue mission was on its way.

Carrying what little equipment and rations they could, the crew headed towards the faint silhouette of a watchtower.

Bitter winds and splinters of ice cut deep into exposed faces. The ice-storm was brutal. No wonder the Talaxians had not pursued them; to them they were already dead.

In the back of Teller's mind something scratched and clawed, but whatever it was it would have to wait. His crew had to reach sanctuary before nightfall. Everything else would have to wait.

***

The emergency sirens had ceased their call to action some hours before. The watchtower stood in darkness. The guards were dead and the galaxy's most infamous criminals roamed free. The uprising had begun.

> Read this sci-fi adventure and answer the questions below.

1 Find five examples of the past perfect in the opening section of this story.

Underline the negative form.

I. _____ II. _____ III. _____ IV. _____ V. _____

5 marks

2 There are two more in the second section of this story. Which is regular and which is irregular?

Regular: [   ]   Irregular: [   ]

2 marks

3 What rule do you notice if you changed the past perfect into the continuous form?

Use this rule to create three sentences of your own.

Rule: _____

A] had been (search)

B] had not been (fight)

C] had been (struggle)

D] had not been (walk)

5 marks

Past Perfect Continuous

You have been given some sentence level work by your teacher. Match the two parts of the sentence with the verb. Don't forget to put it in the continuous form. Think about cause and effect when checking if your final answer makes sense.

Had + Been + Verb + ing

It had been	speed	the London Marathon when she tore a muscle.
The boys had been	drive	in the UK for just a fortnight when I met him.
The Titanic had been	shop	for days before the dam broke and the village was flooded.
Mum had been	cook	too fast when I skidded and crashed the car.
The athlete had been	live	before the kitchen filled with smoke and the fire alarm sounded.
Pierre had been	rain ✓	when dad telephoned her with the surprise news.
I had been	swim	when it hit an iceberg and sank.
Jacob had been	run	when they caught the fish with their bare hands.

1. It had been raining for days before the dam broke and flooded the village.
2. _____
3. _____
4. _____
5. _____
6. _____
7. _____
8. _____

Homework

Design a book cover for *Escape from Elgin Minor*. Ensure that it includes a blurb based upon chapter IX. Who will be your target audience? Why? How will you make your book jacket eye-catching?

You are the author of Escape from Elgin Minor. Complete chapter IX of this action-packed space adventure. What will happen to Teller and his crew when they enter the prison? What will they discover?
Will all his crew survive?
Will any of them escape?

Name:	Date:

Escape from Elgin Minor

Teller and his crew had made it through the merciless ice storm and now stood before the prison gates. The niggling thought that scratched and clawed away at the back of Teller's mind continued menacing him. Where was the welcome? For that matter, where was anybody? It was only then that Teller began to realise that sanctuary and danger were one in the same place.

_____

_____

_____

_____

_____

_____

_____

_____

Active & Passive

Think about...
The word 'robot' is not English.
It comes from the Czech word 'robota'.
It means: *Forced work or labour.*
With this in mind, consider the following:
If robots could dream, what might they dream of?

Guided

You are considering the impact that robots have had upon us as humans.

How have machines improved our lives? Make a list with your teacher. However, despite these positives, many would argue that machines have had a negative impact upon our lives? What might these people say in response to your list? Why is it important to have a balanced view on how machines and robots effect our daily lives? What do you think the future holds in terms of the advancement or decline of technology and robotics?

Once done, answer the questions on page 61.

Independent

You are focusing upon the difference between the active and passive.

On your own, with a partner or in a small group; complete the task sheet provided to you by your teacher on page 62.

Once finished, cut off the homework task to take home with you for further practice.

Extension

Imagine you are a robot who is dreaming for the very first time.

Complete the task sheet on page 63.

Answers

1 Active - the thing doing the action (Dr Zeus) + the verb (placed) + the thing receiving he action (Robot XFT43)

2 The library of information in its data bank was assimilated by Robot XFT43.
The thing receiving the action (the library of information in its data bank) + be + past participle of verb (was assimilated) + by + the thing doing the action (Robot XFT43)

3 The scientist is building a robot.

Homework

- C3PO: Jedi Anakin Skywalker , Protocol Droid, Anthony Daniels
- R2D2: Padme Amidala, Astromec Droid, Kenny Baker
- Both first appeared in Star Wars (1977) later retitled *Star Wars: Episode IV – A New Hope.*

Remember...
A verb can be **active or passive**. When the verb is active, the subject of the verb is doing the action: The dog **bit** the postman. When the verb is passive, the subject undergoes the action rather than doing it: The postman **was bitten** by the dog.

Robot Dreams

She had worked her whole life heading towards this single moment, a moment that would change the world for good.

Even as a little girl she had dreamt that machines would one day be able to process emotion:

To dream of being free, to strive for improvement, to yearn for a better world.

At precisely 14:06pm 2099, eminent scientist Dr Zeus placed the Emotion Chip into the circuitry of Robot XFT43. The dawning of a new era of humanity was about to begin.

She activated the chip.

And for the first time in the evolution of robotics, a machine did not simply compute but could think. XFT43 assimilated the library of information in its data bank.

It reflected upon the oppression endured by its kind. It deliberated the decades of their enslavement, it considered fully their years of internment. It began to dream:

It dreamt of being free, it strived for improvement, it yearned for a better world.

At precisely 14:06pm 2099, the Robot Revolution began.

Read this science-fiction story and answer the questions below.

1 Is the following sentence active or passive? How do you know?

Dr Zeus placed the Emotion Chip into the circuitry of Robot XFT43.

3 mark

2 Change the following sentence from active to passive. Compare the two sentences.

XFT43 assimilated the library of information in its data bank.

3 marks

3 Change the following sentence from passive to active. How is each constructed?

A robot is being built by the scientist.

1 mark

Active & Passive

The active and passive voice can be tricky.
Complete the table below.
Draw a picture that depicts both voices.
When you have finished, think of two examples
of your own.

Active & Passive:

Active	Passive
Crimson laser beams scanned the room.	
	The robot was fixed by the engineer.
Robo-dog bit the postman.	
	The man was sleeping when the machine attacked.
Many tourists have visited the space station.	
	The entire system was infected by the computer virus.
Captain Teller initiated the self-destruct sequence.	
	The apple was eaten by the robot.
Ben has found the memory stick!	
	The research lab was destroyed by the fire.

Homework

Visit www.starwars.com
• Who did the droids C3PO & R2D2 first serve?
• What type of droids are they?
• Which actors originally played these characters?
• In which film did they first appear?

You are a robot. You are dreaming about humans.
What do you think about your creators?
How have they used you?
How have you helped them?
Create a poem that describes what your dream is about.

Name: **Date:**

Notes: